membery

PKRajput

In *membery*, Preeti Kaur Rajpal uses the tool of memory towards her own articulation of language. She writes through post-memory, that is, the memory of the generations after a great human calamity imparted to them through family and community story-telling, materials, silences, and spiritual practice. She uses post-memory to describe her grandparents' experiences of violent expulsion from their homeland during Historical India's Partition. She braids this with her own and her family's experiences as Sikhs in America during the post-9/11 era, a time of increased racialization of Sikhs. Through these subjects, she renders a poetry which explores memory's communal functions — how memory can make one a part of and also how it can sever apart membership from nationhood, the family, and even within the self.

The poet writes of birhaan, the pain of separation from the divine, as understood in the Sikh tradition, used as a metaphor for the griefs and losses explored through history. These histories span from monumental moments of global consequence to small awakenings in the poet's childhood.

In *membery*, the poet proceeds on her own odyssey for a vernacular, set within her acquisition of the Punjabi script of Gurmukhi. The poet searches for a place of articulation, as the poet learns of a larger, more personal dialect aware to the world — its separations and its divisions. Formally daring and lyrical, the poems of *membery* weave memory, Sikh spiritual tradition, family, country, and language acquisition as they forge the author's own language.

Preeti Kaur Rajpal expertly frames poetry as a space particularly conducive to conversation between artistic traditions, genres, and types of rhetoric. But this capacious book is not simply a tribute to modernist influence. Rajpal places experimental technique and its array of forms — including templates that are not germane to poetry, footnotes, and hybrid texts — in dialogue with religious texts, urgent human rights issues, and nonwestern philosophy. In such a way, Rajpal forges a complex, multifaceted poetics of social justice. Indeed, she reveals literature as a hypothetical testing ground, where language is no longer constrained by categories or genres, and this fluidity can give rise to new — and more ethical ways — of moving through the world. Here, the poetic text is revealed as intervention, as corrective gesture, as reversal. *membery* is the kind of book that takes up residence in one's memory.

membery

Preeti Kaur Rajpal

Tupelo Press
North Adams, MA

membery
Copyright © 2023 Preeti Kaur Rajpal

ISBN: 978-1-946482-98-3 (paperback)

Library of Congress Control Number: 2023021425
Cataloging-in-Publication data available on request.

Cover and text designed by Allison O'Keefe.

Cover art: Arpana Caur, Stepping Out (2000). Oil on canvas, 5 x 7 ft.
© Arpana Caur. Used by permission of the artist.

Handwritten Gurmukhi alphabet by Ranjit Singh Rajpal. Used by permission.

First paperback edition November 2023

Tupelo Press
P.O. Box 1767
North Adams, Massachusetts 01247
(413) 664-9611 / Fax: (413) 664-9711
editor@tupelopress.org / www.tupelopress.org

Tupelo Press is an award-winning independent literary press that publishes fine fiction, non-fiction, and poetry in books that are a joy to hold as well as read. Tupelo Press is a registered 501(c)(3) non-profit organization, and we rely on public support to carry out our mission of publishing extraordinary work that may be outside the realm of the large commercial publishers. Financial donations are welcome and are tax deductible.

This project is supported in part by the National Endowment for the Arts.

for my parents

The Age of Kaljug is like a knife. — Guru Nanak Dev Ji

* * *

I am a stranger
learning to worship the strangers
around me

whoever you are
whoever I may become

— June Jordan

contents

manglacharan   1

the first udaasi

ੴ   5

the second udaasi

the place of articulation   9

ecdysis I-III   10

counting your stars in patiala   14

watching the wagah   15

the spinning wheel   16

when the tiger presents itself   17

the second language   20

counting your stairs in patiala   21

the third udaasi

the last rites   25

the negotiations   27

the ticking   28

the singing   30

the cleansing   32

the archive   34

the capture   38

the excision   40

the fall   41

the wall   44

the disarticulation   47

the fourth udaasi

PATRIOT ACT, MISCELLANEOUS   51

ecdysis IV   78

the fifth udaasi

the scent of a s|l|i|c|e|d orange lingers   81

summer nocturne   82

the teething   84

the second thief   86

insectarium   87

dustsceawung   88

counting our lice in patiala   89

aphasia   91

haas   93

lafz   94

notes   97

previous publications   101

acknowledgements   103

about the author   105

manglacharan

ଥ

first guard at the gate
majuscule to adorn
              the one

soapstone to my lips
the mouth's carving
opening my hollow

the first udaasi

ੳ

my first language falls
from the uncoiling jute ladder
of my father's mouth
ੳ ੳੜ my father teaches
oora ooth i repeat the song
to flood my own red river

ੳ

earliest tongue traveler
carrying the nectar of each
book's page the ruby gourd
shaking seed into the eternal
music of my terracotta
vase lettering the Guru

my alphabet's trowel
ੳ the first to be murmured

with ੳੜ the camel
cloven hoof imprint
in the reddening sand
when i lose my gallop

vowel handwritten
in the form of formless
ink humps brimming
rosewater the calligrapher
drinks through the night
layered letter cloaked
in the wool of opening
the camelback's fat cells
asters within this lingual mirage
spilling deluge of first script
through my hulled breath
a sesame seed in time

the pen etching origin

in ੪ the shape of a sickle's
blade hooking the silken
wheat field the rippling
gold snake thread reaping
the paper-skinned drum

with a steel spoon to draw
a double-beat while women
sing wedding songs i clutch
the alphabet saddle's rein
the stave tied down with brass
nails of my empire's splitting

ੲ
the beginning
how one enters
the door knowing
there will be an exit

the second udaasi

the place of articulation

in throated summer we reign over my grandparents to enter patiala humid
under curfew sneaking our rented ambassador of green american children
past police checkpoints while the heaving saavan sky bribes a tin monsoon
mosquitoes drone in raag of malhar as our clean-gilled grandmother marches
us to the whirled toilet when we complain of our tummies the waterborne
disease and country *ghussalkhaana* she orders we repeat the foreign croaking
our limited tongues press backs of our throats from the root lifting to our soft
palates under roof of thought home of far-mouth guttural songs where frogs live
just as we children found the frogs glot-glotting from their own throats
leaping on the marble verandah as rain tirip-tiripped the slipping floor
while my auntie ran for the dripping trousers drying on a rusted clothesline
at last alone and the croaking grown we race to the ghussalkhaana to grab
our grandmother's private turquoise bathing bucket though she forbid her dirty
darlings to even touch the wash-bucket but we americans steal it under cover
of jhim-jhim we fill the pail with spigot water as the wind and ocean gather
a rain of frogs in our grandmother's holy plastic playing against her pale
rules with a ring of long-legged swimmers circling in our bucket pool as open
gutters around the outer-walls flood with sewage we children cup our hands
to catch the jumping water singing as it falls back into the river of laughing
frogs in a pounding kin-minh as our webbed feet circumambulate our divine

ecdysis

I

dinner tonight i warm my father
rajma chaval in rusty microwave
emitting zap-dusted radiation stars

red kidneys hiss spices sizzling flesh
hai Rabba! i step back swallow my tongue
before anyone accuses me lazy

daughter-duty excuses i peek
the top microwave grates *saap! saap! a snake!*
shaken faqir fallen from attic magic

mouse chute slipped in all chance silk garden
snake but we imagine him gold fortune
teller trance rattler flute charmer eternal

contortionist my father and i
share the same burning nightmare falling
into the dimmed well of snakes i sometimes see

the nightmare necklaced night after night
in the glittered morning we count thousands
poisons fangs gilded serpent eyes flicking tips   o! how we escaped!

my father's tongue language forked arrow
compass he taught me to trace gurmukhi
script before english our punjabi shooting

continuous long letters slither
leather skin shedding high curves coils writhing
 lines knots alphabets twisting amongst themselves

their own pit

II

rainy days my mother teaches me
to play 'snakes and ladders' though umreekan
games come cartoon-flat destined in cardboard

tiles christened starless 'chutes and ladders'
o! i cherished the die! the die! to chance
throw spit small ivory teeth their onyx sheen

flush cheeks in golden descent sidewind
sliding down a snake's spiral spine rapt tiled
falling five thieves kaam khrod lobh moh haankar hot

in my hands so early heat-sensing
organ preying young prayer then to be
a woman walk down the ophidian street

late at night a strange man pulling out
his snake next morning i identify
him in a zigged line-up i choose the arab

looking man though the police corrects
me *sorry   miss   wrong   we suspect   this man*
serpens caput captured he points to a white

man his reptile eyes pair of scythed dice
i have swallowed the boiled venom this country
shimmering skins weighing scale iridescence   my father

wears the tallest turban bombs will fall
across euphrates striking in six months
i don't know the compression of what will come

the drummed go-back-to-your-country snare
cold-blooded snake split dripped his open flares
 hilting shovel beating his gold-hammered head flat

when he is forced underground

III

under sky of opal-eyed stars i snake
my liver clean of thirst with bottlebrush tree's bristles
kaleja the liver avatar of heart circling

language of my feet their incarnations
winged naaga in skin of love desire madness to talk
to the ambered moon yellowing tooth of an old snake

under stars spectacle-eye wonder why
Waheguru? why didn't i scale the red ladder?
why is the Beloved's home still a distant clay lamp?

why did i roll the sinking pyre die slide
to square-one the board flat-lucked under my urned stars
i play the stars descending the flute's scales choosing the key

my father remembers his own gold
bangled mother watched to track the burning oil night
in dada siba after the new skein government

relocates the family into hidden
mountains once caravans of millions snaked across
a bloody border striking august heat under threats

pits of snakes guns knives gilt molting country
there are no hooded cobras here like the coiled king
my grandmother found under my father's bed one night

i walk through the dark

bare foot

counting your stars in patiala

the air boils the flighted summer we touch down patiala
our forewings and hindwings unfold their child lines
a swarm of cousins parents and grandparents sleep
on the rooftop a long row of hand-loomed white sheets
lain flat the roof like paper our own night bureaucracy
judging who will slumber next to whose gossiping snore

once we tuck ourselves in our sheets small folded envelopes
on the officer's desk we count stars the whole night naming
the nameless galaxies pointing to the bright where dead
saints now live at dawn we awake covered in fat flies
the constellations descend upon our skin into our open
mouths we children shoo off the flies their angry buzzing
their mourning their green black shimmering resin
their feet dipped in the open sewers outside the home

flies fly body to body as we lay in first light's mortuary
their emerald hulls full of life its leaves and hums
rubbing their thin hands together in prayer or plotting
these small gods of death and their unforgiving maggots
we american children flap our sheets shuffling entry papers
to this hour of quiet like the ears of elephants fanning insects
clearing our giant bodies while the adults chant morning
prayers and name the dawn Waheguru Waheguru Waheguru

my grandfather's toes curl from under his sheet of exile
all the constellations sit unbothered on his body *why* we ask
do you let the flies sit on you? we children hover over him giggling
at what old age can undo he tells us *they have to sit somewhere*
we all have to home somewhere the flies their thousands of eyes
thousands of flying stars watching thousands vanishing into the light

watching the wagah

at the border closing ceremony peacocks
soldiers kick legs up scissor air rifles click
for the wired border an old shrine of steam
kites of neighbor children fly back and forth
the wires by thread a blade in their fingers
under the splitting august heat's only sun
in the VIP tourist booth under voltaic fans
cut last minute from a scored paper map
the idols stretch their spines in anthems
the regiments howl nation with the golden
an electric orange blood running nuclear
her ash remains in the border's shadow hot
over the grand trunk road's shifting sands
the border crosses me and i unable to cross
i whisper *Waheguru* who holds the spooled
my flock's dust membered by 1947's dusk
steel gates pulled down like knives at sunset

strut flayed parade in turbans khaki salute
the countries' teacups clack cheer in turn
spills over the barbed fence as thin paper
slitting the sky into strips each side slices
i sit sweating with the indians a daughter
red instead of with the sun-burnt americans
the circus tent locked in radcliffe's line
unfolding fate in the twist of rotating guards
hoisting their incense onto the rising wall
jackals grazing the capitols in alloy glimmer
through my mother's grandmother's wrists
loo blows her ground bone into my hands
the two flags rise and fall like a final breath
inherit the spinning wheel a beating retreat
string between the door from Ram to Allah
pigeons in flight who wing the impassable
the eternal light's name scattering in half

the spinning wheel

i never learn how to spin
cloth but i can hear Bhagat
Kabir singing to his spinning
wheel the charkha repeating
hundreds and hundreds of names
for Rabb while the spokes circle
a crimsoned cotton Bhagat Kabir
winding his own strings of grief
into the separated threads woven
taut across the spindles of time

in our backyard sandbox my sister conductor
shouts *hold tight!* our red merry-go-round spins
she digs her jelly-sandaled foot into the ground
i clutch the rails as we twirl two wooden tops
on a dizzy earth our dresses rise sorrow in the air
sand pellets our arms and legs flying in a blur
we bite our tongues tasting first blood of birhaan
as we bury our childhood in sunset's blanket

inside our mother lays on a couch in the living
room she weaves a new garment her own mother
just arrived in the country yet lost in an american
hospital needles and gut thread into her belly over
and over the stomach sore in plaits we ribbon sisters
hear our mother singing to a cracked wheel in raag
gauri bairaagan she wears a winter shawl of dried
pomegranate peel outside we unravel the rust veil
we chase our own ruddy speed of sound shrieking
through our self-created torque our girlhood high
pitch our long braids flying straight out unspooling

o Kabir let me hear you warp
and weft a mother wrapped in cloth
dyed in a red which will not bleed

when the tiger presents itself

before i am born a tiger
is lost in the new burning

city my grandfather searches each
train station for his disappeared

face his face printed on plastered
posters hung on boards for the missing

in the new city he visits the chlorinated
hospital asking for any news good

or bad winter fog prowling the cold
emptied carriages circling the walls brick

rising to divide a man into a country
setting fire-traps and hatch snares

smoke plumes offer themselves as guides
to the road tailing out to the uncut forest

its green laws of how to live without
encroaching on the tiger's territory

the map bleeds in lures of civility
the new city's flower shops bursting

sons hand-picked roses arcing headless
without petals red pulp a part of a man

in my own time of growing endangered
the wide window spills clawed photos air

raids under night vision flickering green
animal eyes and camo men greened

tactical in the walls of a lit day the rose
stems escaping copper long range neon

green lights shooting across the line
a foreign sky captured in the television

while a newscaster introduces a country
new to me my own its fangs tearing

flesh and the far gotten country a green
zone umbra of prisons rising renditions

night ballads unsung by the burled
blindfold wearing captivity's orange

flame folded on haunches behind stripes
of cages in daylight furring with the living

tigers in this country where i am a magician
seeing the tiger and then not seeing the tiger

the next minute disappearing a man
into the son smolder of a black box

from this pit of smoke i conjure
my grandfather and i ask him

shadowstriped *what did you do*
when you found the tiger? what

should i offer the man-eater
his mouth stalking me everywhere?

he tells me *i fed him what he hungered*
i gave my head into the darkness

in exchange the tiger gave me all the missing
parts of myself and a map to the new city

the second language

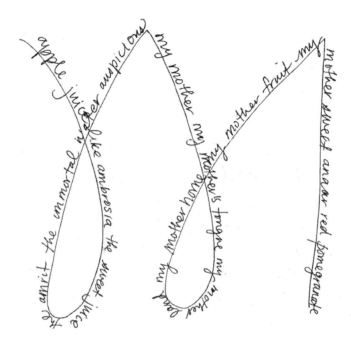

and

at first bite in the fleshed apple of language i am abloom in alphabet
blessed ਅ as the second letter an areola to my mouth's august armor
cooing ਅ ਅਨਾਰ ਅ *anaar* pomegranate's awning i learn our amaranthine
door to speech ਅ ਅਨਾਰ as 'a is for apple' amplified in the absence of
english i laugh at the sour apple slices i offer my acidic american tongue
fooled into absolution's aura which instead aches for an always undying
guru's amrit an abiding avalanche of amethyst arils lined in my aorta
her halved archives of ambrosial anatomies within the inarticulate
i appeal to the ambered letter-carrier why the apple in an alien world
judging adam argil of aadmi his acts an affliction instead i answer aperture
kissed by the harvester who beheads anaar from the aster tree of aurat
left to right splitting a second alphabet the aureate amulet i adorn
my mother's tongue imprinting an argot alive to all the reddening

counting your stairs in patiala

i am thirteen and clean my grandfather's
room bed wooden molding plaster walls

i fold a white sheet wool grey blanket no tassels
who are you he asks each corner tucked distance

i dust a dead bulb hanging between light
winter always lahore here patiala fifty years

since border cracked whip fenced sparrows
crossing flocks heads cut off pouring bodies

arrive dismembered last train on the shelf i find
an aana coin from the other side i ask *what could it buy*

once? a sack of rice he says *who are you to touch* i split
quiet open his one book carried over the line 'richard yea

& nay' he strings his grade-13 gora english teacher's
voice repeating whip accent the gora caning the class

your grandfather is your grandfather
yea or nay your grandfather is yea or nay

yea: a pyjama-type his tallness turban beard
nay: a pantaloon-type stamped ledger pages

i find money my grandmother was missing
hidden in pages in case the earth slivers another

season's cleaning i collect crinkled notes
dried on metal hanging-line gathered from open

sewer outside the house we forgive him
neighbors laugh when he stands naked

on the verandah flies refuge on his body
always in a past he grabs me tight by wrist

my eight-boned banyan hammering radius and ulna
ending together a closed umbrella *who are you what*

are you throwing his own papers *get out* my grandfather
is never my grandfather is always in this perched room

a paper-lined bird's nest i remember my grandfather
climb down the staircase descending into his own

solitude thirteen steps from his sky i hold his hand
as he counts each step like Guru Nanak counted

the grain on the scale on and on an unending rain
beyond the stone of exchange the great partition

between you and Yours recounted thirteen in my
language tera in his language meaning yours   *Ik*

he counts each step *do tin chaar panj che*
saath aath nau das gyaara baara tera

Tera Tera Tera Tera the border fading between us
Tera hee Tera Only Yours Only Yours the balance

toppling the heavied nest in me towards the line
a canopy of memory opening against a bone rain

the third udaasi

the last rites

in the langar kitchen off highway 99
once we chop onions and our knives
sleep we throw the cubes of light
into a steel pot where a chariot boils

the room steams in a fog of woman
gaggle rolling death dough lies
before us a sheet our heads covered
in cloth of final prayer i pinch

the atta rolls small grandmothers
in my hands i pass the old bodies
to other women in line slapping
clapping flipping rolling throwing

flat onto the gas flame the room green
in hum of someone else's grandmother
puffing full of air tapping her knuckles
overseeing the unlearned stacks of round

roti to feed the still hungering
on a saturday close to cremation
my grandmother just become
whole after living her whole

life adhoora a part of a self
now her light poora whole
returned into the steel circle
the kara pulsing my wrist

in this langar kitchen a girl melts
butter rubs hundreds like i learnt
to be blood her long braids jumping
ropes inside memory outside highway

99 roars the smog split by red rows
of oleander big-rig oxen moaning
metal hauling cargo between fragment
while inside a lucky man on asylum

stirs a vat of milk in the corner his arms
engine and turban loosens the bubbling
we recite the boatsman's name ferrying
us strangers into a next light we take turns

peddling cracked wooden oar we race
the clot curdling acid thick flesh form
from formless last procession in this boiling
land neither lok nor parlok but the trial

of a whole vessel a flame flicks the man's
half thumb his stub singes green char filling
the room's mouths all punjab's police left
when the blades awakened the countryside

the bodies disappearing

                              like bread

the negotiations

under the light of homeland a war the silhouette
of unlistening punches my brother his turban bare
his hair unraveling america again at its red alert door
we petition the university authority for a passage of entry
to the dotted line of papered promise our men pulled
from the dream in the green haze of an unnamed war
when the talks begin i enter the negotiations on their terms
in raghead genie camel-jockey terrorist osama arrows aimed
for men but in the time of negotiation i become a woman
shrouded in chiffon i retreat to the kitchen i boil water endless
i join my mother in steam wonder what side of the condemning
we sit at our own long table among yesterday's dishes souring
we breathe stale air eat dust and cook in absolution hush our self
questionnaires we make lists of grocery-wants and unwanted
we stare at each other's strange face bargained into someone else's

until we gasp shattering the porcelain plates lined in gold leaf
our bellies shake out the swallowed feathers of compromise

                                                    we   e x p l o d e

we laugh
and laugh

we hiss

we haa

we know what will come again

                        we have found

                                    our way

                                                out

the ticking

i keep my grandfather's international red
cross card in case the soldier lost to war
in an enemy country in the old echoing
drawer i keep the sleeping watches which lost

their ticking in the world war feathering
the family record in my dresser the dead
faces their missed deadlines crossings final
arrivals unknown in my limbic land maybe

misr maybe iraq burma maybe his name in a field
surgeon operative guide i do not wear history
by arm but someday i will place my pointing
on the brits' pulse their records wrist belonging

in the scroll of dismembering i will ask *my blood?*
where seen? where? my blood's scene? my blood?
did see the others bleed? the drawer of my halved
memory opened by an iron hand's rasp of blood

when the brits' exact archive answers me half
truths in their tea accent *what wrist do not risk*
arrest wrest belonging we do not hold hands
no record of his time or after the dawning

i will draw my own face on the clock setting
to the blood hour the crown pulled out the socket
the unmetering minute falling behind glass
a second hand marching the soldier home

crimson parting my grandfather's own blood sliced
clean in the wake their infidel faces unable to escape
belief or hide Akal's gold brick in a turban unraveling
still in my ram's horn the red hour's striking hand

hurling upon me to unscrew the missing face
of unsearched belief into the lost sand's nameless
pulse its unknown facts and family lore the even
drum of darkness its measures and disappearance

the singing

with our child-eyes small insects smashed
against the glass of our san joaquin kitchen

we peek the window while all the women
of the house hiss and tell us he is gone

baba gaya! my grandmother squawks
red hot *don't look!* my mother shrieks

a bird cursing my father for his father
our child-wings still perched on the tree

of innocence my grandfather lays alone
humming himself under the mulberry's

canopy he is naked wearing the final
garment excavating his own clay vase

as if from harappa's ruins singing an ancient
song of partitions under the sun the mulberries

bodies sweetening as dark star clusters
small black crows flocked together august

berries swelling under the conquering heat
until they fall my grandfather calls the fruit

shahtoot a berry royal fit for a king a name
carried over mountain range on horseback

and arrow the lost words travel sticky blood
in my grandfather's head his leaves quivering

the plaques flutter as buried constellations
entombed in my grandfather's red birdcage

the trains crossing the killings the falling
bodies the mulberries' stain seeping the land

alone he swallows an entire constellation
branched on the back of his throat the crows

sweep up my grandfather into Ajrael's empire
where the flight sings their song of separation

we listen to him all afternoon as his song splatters
bleeding into the earth our nestled silkworms spinning

the cleansing

i climb the stone of my father's seven
days of white undershirts the himalayan

snow caps and his pyjamas the cobalt
of satluj river i separate time's mountain

from running water and fill the washing
machine with soap the drum a tumbling

week full of my father's yellow yolk
sweat stains which hang beneath his arms

i untangle the clutch of shirts a ground nest
of bar-headed geese eggs only one survives

i watch the birds swoosh and swash spume
through glass suds curdling like sunday

child hair-baths our heads mother-scrubbed
from the playground sand then sun-dried

hair hanging to our knees mustard oil kneaded
by her knuckles crowning our feather scalps

after the bell rings i pull out the bodies stuff
the spun migrants into the dryer's belly steam

drifts as the trains swell on the last day
the bloody raj a stranger pushes my dada

onto the last train before the thin garment
of country births itself tears out the arms

by the long threads of their own seams
afterwards i grab each warm day by chest

lay down the belly flat like the nation's paper
headlines the purge how my dadi pressed her

pregnant stomach swollen with my father
praying her mountain flat running the hills

drinking detergent refusing dinner cutting off
one more refugee's child before the dirt world

in a land cleaned of elbows i fold the shoulders
away like my dada's hunched back someday

my father will also be a small man
i want to remember him unwashed

by the killings a daily coronation
of ivory soap anointing in pepper

cologne and simco fixo gluing his face
hair to his chin-skin holding his beard black

the archive

specimen: the missing

in the backlight of history i search
the road to partition archive its torn
digital ledgers index of brittle speeches
catalogs of the cracked clay colony
i unbury the bronze ox of my finger
clicking the camps sun temples crumble
in my headphones as i listen to files
radio broadcasts sweeping in and out
of the lacquer grooves pigeons skittering
in flight between seeds of blighty i scan
yellow-greened fragments decreeing NO
to the bisection of wings the map a scrap
of the vetting my eyes glow like moths
inking lineage as i flit the endless bright
trapped in the scrolling myth of cinder

i garland in this bodiless caravan
still smoldering bone trailing pyre
the screen buzzes in operation
of legacy burning 47's disappeared

history's halo flickers my halved discoveries
i drag my finger to transfer a queen's viceroy
from british to our punjabi hands i warble
ascension into the missing pages in the scorching
my throat plumes as a babiha before the deluge
i sing prio-prio prio-prio a rainbird's song
summoning monsoon in the beloved's absence

from my own beak i sanctum into the swarm
the sky a soot record of birdshot and exodus
i unearth birhaan here between the separation
of memory i touch the bonfire and i become

a poet

i write my own partition
from the shredding documents
lit feathers by history's can of black oil

secondary source:

sitting like a comma
in the war years
i search history

i open another window to my falling
silicon shock and awe i read the times
reloading the gossamer lies i control
alt delete and fill a darkened forest
of commission reports with my solitaire
the distracted decks descend night
invasion burning the screen's disbelief
the state's files disappear half-lives
of memory a box rises and i accept
i strike the head of the red match
on the bonfire of my own preservation

i too
in the smoke
of overwriting
memory

my own archive
ignited

primary source:

years before
when my grandfather races green
country's sludge by a last train
he flies over the midnight fence
with a broken wing our blood
set on the bullock cart's wheel
lahore to amritsar screeching
bird whistles

all he carries with him is name

once arrived in the camps his body
out of his own body he cooks himself
roti on an iron tava the flame churns
butter lighting his long beard to clutch
his head he bends into his immolation
searching the burning with the glimmed
eyes of Chitr Gupt the final recorders
who report to Yama's swallowing empire

my grandfather lowers his forehead
to the steel plate of his own light

he reads what is written
in the cracked wheat
then eats of himself
what remains
after the embering

the capture

i descend into the dark halls
climbing down the concrete
stories of my university library
the subterranean air swamps
dry icehusk within the vault
filled with old laws of quiet
mildew colonizes the air
as spores scatter my gaping

i pass a sign *all who enter*
here must keep their quiet
books clothed in silken
history moan from the shelves
voices of headless pigeons
pierce a glass subcontinent
of dust its roaming caravans
a dead bird's stench hovers

the books a partition museum
of loot ferrying beasts of forced
famines on display in collection
with a sculpted stone re-telling
of narsingh's battle familiar
as a grandfather in a turban
half man half lion captured
in a hell labeled provenance

i pull out a book on the census
its half truths and lies of counting
wrapped in the white bark of grand
trunk eucalyptus its infected stem
cankers and leaves of gall tattered
cotton cloth zeroes lined up in each
molding book of dead i smudge
their sulphur residue on my forehead

i run my fingers through annexation
kings and their ruin sons exiled
in faded garb the deeds signed
away in empire's gunpowder
as the recitations of Yama's century
release as river from colonial dam
nation in the archive's landless castes
mouths stuffed shut like book lice

as silent as the women who fell over
and over into wells without language
handing over the book of themselves
when i first hear my breath disappears
like when i see the body in a glass cage
Guru Granth Sahib split naked and seized
without even a brocade eyelash yet trapped
in a ninth circle of enlightenment its gangrene
neon flickering glare on the festering spoils

the excision

after the surgeons cut out the tumor
the pathologist shows me my mother's
       lung *do you want to hold it?*
       i want to hold her unopened
       green mottled emigrant wing
       flight before scalpel and after

her left lower lobule sliced chest
her five rivered breath karaamat
       her pleura atoned miracle a non-believer's membrane
       her inhale a palm pushing the hurled boulder of dome
       like Guru Nanak's five-finger imprint in time's stone
       her exhale defiant a pir to spring her own holy water

the pathologist a victor wrapped
in the cocoon of surgical greens
       points out the grey jewel all 186 carats mountain
       of light our koh-i-noor sitting in the english
       crown alone someday overthrown i will steal
       back our diamond our land and mothers

i have no faith in the long life lines
of my palms under a living room
       light their stone-clear revelations slipping
       when my mother reads my scraped future
       from my hands gripping the most human
       parts of me my fingers and their opposition

this tumor told no secrets despite the operating
room's lamp on the ridgelines of her cauterized
       country drifting blueprints in the hands
       of foreign growths rifting the creator
       her mothername her motherbody
       you can lose to such quiet shapes

                i hold my mother's breath

the fall

before i learn to read
the lengthening shadows
i learn november is a month
without roses all the red
bells of the garden quiet

the school bus distant
i ask my nani what red
gem shall i take my teacher
plucking the yard of morning
she twists the star of anaar

i brim a brown paper bag
with a heap of pomegranate
though i do not know how
to say the long perishing
in a red-blooded english

i am good with words now i am
good with knives too slitting open
a pomegranate seeded burnt apple
i shake the one thousand flaming
tongues falling into a glass bowl

filling the cup with the red
balloon cutting autumn's night
i stain my hands dark in the glove
with the sap of memory juiced
from my grandmother's fall

my mother drinks this nectar
of grief still tries to be a mother
when my milk teeth fall out
my mother collects each duff
tooth into a gilded pill box

she finds me behind the tree
hiding-and-seeking my mother
shakes my mouth's treasure
tells me a troupe of tiny elephants
rattles in my gold box of loss

i sleep now with an ivory
army marching my mouth
i taste the blood of their trampling
i cut this fruit like a child made
of petals as the frost descends

i only see the pink button camellia
the last bow blooming my own
pink frock the red's shadow fading
for the first time not a single yard
rose in the border of november

i have not forgotten my nani
walking me to the bus shaking
the bag filled with anaar my teeth
hollowing loose my pronunciation
the pomegranates bursting orchestra

each winter a death i return
to this body in a new life
san joaquin tule fog blankets
the ground covered in a red
mouth i see and cannot see

december darkens my grandmother
kisses me and dies again in america
a hospital alone a drug interaction
my mother's mother's velvet stomach
lining tearing my mother's last flower

setting the family on fire

                    a red fruit

the wall

in the house of language
a wall i cannot translate
rises from the fire hidden
within returning matarisvan
i climb the mother-brick
altar born of mud-picked
rivers air sigh sun-dry
the earth's high flame

the brick belonging
to the red beginning
language of my own
mother's mother my biji
her everlasting name
Ishar the highest being
is also a grandmother
Ishar beginning in ੲ
the third letter of languish
i learn as brick ੲ ਇੱਠ

i remember after crossing
the pacific swell my biji
grandmothers like a brick
she gifts us piles of steel
plates etched with the heft
of our sikh names at night
she reads the bricks of time
magazines piled in the living
room on sundays she clicks
tongue at my mother's cooking
instead fries stacks of garden
gourds my mother's mother's
bricks a lick of her survives
my grandmother in the freezer

biji speaks to me in an Indian
english and i learn from her
how to mold to a shape of grief
my mouth widens to sound
the opening vowel of first death

ੲ a letter bricking brick
ੲ ਇੱਠ a baking bond
ੲ ਇੱਠ brick on brick
ੲ Ishar ੲ Ishar ੲ Ishar
i repeat my new worship
practicing the name in crayon
on the brick fireplace my mother
never learns to light her face
as daughter or as mother

on the day i learn my biji
crosses the longest ocean
water leeches salts of bairaag
on the mortar of my childhood

the bricks rise to build
the wall of my mother
i become a girl too
bricked of an unsaying
a thick brick of loss
laid across my mother
my mother laid across me
brick by brick as wet
as clay cut with the red
thread of Ishar Ishar Ishar
the eternal name pulling
the origin of all origin
back across the wall

when the archeologists
first dug through to harappa
they found the site alone
surrounded by an ancient
wall of fire-baked bricks
building an untouchable
red barrier for the river's
flooding season of grief

i don't remember her body
laid brickwise into an american
hospital then entering the kiln
burning her clay into a red
light i only remember Ishar
the brick of her name eternal

the disarticulation

my wrist ember endless lightburn i tactile
tendon passage way ligament clasp distal
bone tunnel Brahma's name three morning
language palace ossein fixed formalin kin
glinting retinaculum wrapping grand great
father simmer marrow sharp phantom dukh
sever river no manned land carpus rim limb
rain mother dust great grand her red drum
thumb hum column sesamoid sinew singe
radius scalpel spew cartilage ulna joint brood
hand hunt condyloid east-west brick blood
arm flee crescent mob writ blade glim flood
axe haft chop ang back bless bit split rift drift

lahore lunate sargodha scaphoid

      peshawar trapezoid rawalpindi trapezium

            capitate hamate pisiform

                    triquetrum

                        triquetrum

                          triquetrum
                          quickquitrun
                          triquetrum
                          tricksplitone
                          triquetrum
                          triquetrum

the fourth udaasi

PATRIOT ACT, MISCELLANEOUS
(from TITLE X, UNITING AND STRENGTHENING AMERICA BY PROVIDING APPROPRIATE TOOLS REQUIRED TO INTERCEPT AND OBSTRUCT TERRORISM (USA PATRIOT ACT) ACT OF 2001)

1

2

---

1   my grandfather said :: always read the small print

2   sound travels :: all directions

      sound :: to the intended :: sound :: to the unintended

3

4

---

3 miscellaneous, synonyms: sundry,
                              different,
                          many,
                              confused,
                                  disordered,
                                      indiscriminate,
                                          multifarious,
                                              scattered

4 *when the noctambulist falls from the trapeze*

   she falls out of time
   descending through the dream
   she searches the elephantine
   underworld for the red pollen
   a strand of saffron
   in the heap of reddened
   feathers to wake herself

   creating her own sonic boom

52

5

6

---

5   *the inscription*

locate yourself
on the unmappable
within an eighth ocean
paint your fingernails the red
stain of elephant rumblings
the sprawling law
where you are named
to become someone
good
or at least
useful

enter again
into the terrace
of the page
the uncountable
nadir

in your name

6   when country cuts off first phalanges nib
                lawyers write in a patriot's ink
when country slices until meta-phalanges
                lawyers write a patriot's law
when elephants die
                the trunk from which they breathe and drink
                the nectar shrivels from umbilical reasonings
                the bodies disappear

7

8

9

---

7   if a lie means a long nose
    the longest nose would crack a bridge
    braided elephant trunks unraveling
    between the road into the country
    the day after bombs start to fall
    the bridge will cross the longest river
    the six o'clock evening news speaks
    in language of the mahout's mouth

    and whip

8   tonight's news like every night these years
    reports terror: the elephants were crossing the bridge

    blast   a blast   a blastophere
    18 elephants the morula its caverns
    they were just crossing the bridge

9   terror: from proto-indo-european *tre- to shake. *tres- to tremble. among other origins.

10

11

12

---

10   ibid.

11   he said, "when a big tree falls, the earth shakes"
the prime minister died and her son said
her son said   sun said   after four days of killings
sunset   probably before the killings, too

12   an innocent question, really, from page 2: where are you from?

_____

13   *origin story:*

    first there was light
    then there was sound
    then the anhad shabad
    sang the naam

    somewhere it is night and our mother
    reads us as we sleep
    the stories of Guru Nanak

    the janamsaakhi
    the birth of story told to us
    in the long traveling language
    the cardinal directions in words
    of his epic journeys on foot

    we call his travels udaasi
    journeys through the world-ethers
    udaasi which sounds
    like melancholy in punjabi
    udaasi which sounds
    like odyssey in english
    udaasi which means to be
    outside of the home

    an udaasi: how the needle wanders
    through the page: my own stitch
    into eternity: outside: of a home i call
    home: within the law: and its unquiet
    queen: pulling the long boned threads
    of my nana's military coat: the drum trembling
    the hammer hitting the anvil: then stirrup
    then the burning song: vibrating in my ear

the brits gave my grandfather
the gift of miniaturized
Sri Guru Granth Sahib Ji
a golden offering after
he wore the brutish
uniform in the world
war saving sun setting soldiers
their bomb halved arms

my nana's khaki turban soft
and crumpled as sand
serving a queen and her subjects

though my grandfather attended her
parades he also spit on her name

my grandfather kept our Guru
printed into less than a palm
sized Guru wrapped in muzlin
in his officer-issue turban
during the world war
journeying the unknown
countries and patriots
our shabad our word
our war what is bound
to the universe printed
a sesame seed

the brutish
they printed our written
Guru's limbs
small in their own law
so the soldiers could hold
onto their own head in war

our shabad amongst the things he carried

across the borders outside and in
the end wrapped into his own turban
crossing his own

odyssey:

Guru Granth Sahib in life
a text heavier than an elephant
i cannot lift the 1430 limbs
am i a true seeker if i can only lift my own
udaasi papered in an inherited miniature
fitting in the creases of my hand

"always read the small print"
my grandfather said
to my mother after worlding
war then when whirled back
bereft of belonging my vadde carried on
to the new country at midnight's partition

                   the batwara

                        the t a k i n g

away

                                the t e a r i n g

apart   they never spoke

of the tearing   a p a r t

time   no one spoke

a new country of many
languages where no one spoke

odyssey, further:

as a child my mother stole
the miniature Guru on test
days a school child worried
about her own small print
she carried her smalled
sacred in her pocket the good
luck sneaking the small
superstitions of children

when she grew she carried
our miniaturized limbs
to umreeka where we became
half of half
and half
again

she carried everything
in her red pocket i imagine

where we
become

the small print
of another country

¹⁴

¹⁴

¹⁵   ¹⁶

---

14   miniature wargaming :: sometimes played on game boards

15   see footnotes 1-37. a miniature text.

      miniature :: miniaturized :: minority :: minoritized :: to be made minor

16   counterpoint, listen

      listen, for example:
      eruptions below
      from the scattered silence

17

---

17   acousmatic, definition:
     1) a sound or voice operating
       with an unknown source
     2) a reference to pythagorean disciples
       they listened to his lectures for years
       and years and years behind a curtain
       without seeing the source of the voice
     3) a reference to pre-recorded music presented in a venue using loudspeakers
       for example: it is said at camp echo the torture rooms saturated
       with loud music the music repeating on and on
       amplifying

       born in america and i love you

       in the smoke detectors
       listening devices

       the unseen

18

18   but where are you really from? he asked me again on page 40

no w(here)
a place not bound
by time or space

anhad

19

---

19   time zone, definition:
       a zone which observes a uniform standard time
       often a boundary for a time zone
       is the boundary between countries

       often a boundary between the timeless
       country is memory

       in the text i live between simarna and visarna

       simarna
               to remember all
               that brings one
               into the light
       visarna
               to forget
               to live in all that carries one
               into the shadow

       simarna living in the word visarna

       in the language of my own membering

       time zoned, a working definition, in this case:

       where the trial never ends
       the prisoner grows old
       her name is taken from her

20

20   above also reference, the time, the place:

    the time zone when my father carried Guru
    Granth Sahib across the pacific perched
    on his head the guards in the tokyo airport
    bowed their heads no one touched
    no one inspected the greenish
    starjet samsonite carrying the body

    at sight of our Granth
    the guards removed their shoes

                           barefoot

    even then even there the crossing

                                customs

21

21   families hold weddings before first snow
      when people gather some dance some
      dance with shoes some dance barefoot
      arms reach for sky some people hold each
      other's faces to see lakes in each other's eyes
      from sky all lakes look like mirrors from sky
      all miniature a mirror is a militant when it gathers
      with other lakes you cannot trace who a person is
      or what a person is from a bloodied foot if that is all
      that is left

      people joke about babies at weddings

22

---

22   i auscultate the holes in the walls at jallianwala bagh
          a red stethoscope hanging from my ears
                 i listen to the fifth intercostal space
              the apex of a heart in another empire's hands
                     wisconsin Gurdwara   the sound reverberates a familiar hertz

bullet holes blasting through the wall   we could hear   we could hear
   the white supremacist boots   storm through   we could hear
     the diwan amidst the quiet   of prayer
miniature in the exit   door   though   some of us died

what i mean is   there is a logic   to how the bullets
   of massacre arrange   across the document
           a music   a constellation of stars

---

23   see above

24   riddle: what eats the red wood and dies if it drinks water?

25   fire. let me tell you the myth of fire and the seven sisters. the seven sisters, known as krttika, lived together in the sky. they were wed to the rishis. but one day, agni, the fire god, fell in love with krttika. to distract himself from desire, agni roamed the forest. in the forest, he came across svaha, the star zeta tauri, who fell in love with agni. desperate to conquer the fire god's love, svaha disguised herself as krttika. only six of the krttika though, a mistake. agni was pleased with himself for winning over the supposed krttika. in time, under the deception of night, svaha had a child. word traveled that the rishi's wives were the child's mothers. the rishis divorced their wives, except one, who believed every story deserved to be heard. the other krttika were banished from the part of the sky they knew as home and became the constellation krttika. the krttika are also known as the pleiades, in some parts.

notes for tonight when looking into the vault: say the name. call the krttika. their name meaning 'the cutters.' the krttika's flame is a knife. the law of krttika is to cut ties with negativity, the swallowing page of the night sky.

in the darkness, find krttika. look up.

26   *a disarticulation*
    your rationality? rational the law. law? the rational! ration.,,:,,
    s
    s
    s s s s syntax irrational the. irrational what said. the person outside. what citizen is?

    subject object.

    marginalia. miscellenia. verb.
                          member
    class
    to not be heard ///////[

27   pixelated :: pix from picture :: el from element :: pel :: sample ::
    byte :: bit ::   bot :: dot ::   spot ::   see spot run

28   white space   whitened space
            white our mourning   white noise the frequency
                gaining a power
           through the act of its own

:::::::::::: density::::::::::::::

29

---

29   the rogue bull elephant named osama bin laden killed many people in a small village
osama was later shot though officials are unsure if they shot the correct elephant
the destruction of elephant habitat was not listed as a patriot's act

a mistaken identity was how we named the elephant for some time

30   when american bombs fell over iraq ::
within days :: the first to arrive ::
on my e-mail alert :: marked for *sikh* ::
a notice on the bombing of the Gurdwara ::
the Gurdwara memorializing Guru Nanak's visit ::
to baghdad :: on the border of the green zone ::
where Guru Nanak gave his own ::
call to prayer :: reciting the Japji ::

the saakhi says ::
the pir of baghdad known as 'the one who holds the hand' ::
asked the impertinent stranger :: green of green ::
where are you from? :: *what are you here to say?* ::

Guru Nanak spoke :: back to the pir ::
the limitless nethers :: and the limitless sky ::
and in the limitless sky :: the countless languages ::

the entire city of baghdad turned ::
to a quiet gold ::
listening to this migrant ::
who spoke of the four directions::

with no limit

31

---

where are you really from? have you paid your member fee?
where

from   really   where
       are you   wherefrom   do you remember   really areyou   member
from really really really from where where are you   where

32   *the day after the disaster still unfaced*

politicians declare a moment   [   ]

they write the listening law

can you hear the oliphants

the holy ants crawling up the trunk
into the black box

reels of conversation   a woman talking to her lover in hurried breath

the unending records   the s c a t t e r ed
sound

the orange peeling from the prisoner's cell

33

34

---

33   the night raids
      the sound of a nation
      acoustic anechoic chambers

34   her name
      samar hassan
      five years old
      splattered

35

35   pulsatile tinnitus can be caused
     by turbulent blood
     flow in the labyrinthine
     vessels

     the sensation of hearing blood

36 four days after the towers fell
    before shooting balbir singh sodhi five times
    frank roque shouted *i am a patriot*

    patriot, english, an etymology:
    from french, patriote
    and before that
    from latin, patriota
    fellow countryman

    patriot:
    from greek, patriotes

    and before that
    from patrios
    of one's father

    father from pa
    from the baby's mouth
    pather pither pather potter
    creator inventor

    author

37   (earlier the problem was
       the people were known as) a dusky peril

       [when arrested after the next shootings]
       (*of a lebanese-american and an afghan-american)
       frank roque shouted
       i stand for america
       all the way

       in the morning
       on the same day of the murder
       a group of white males yelled
       go back to your
       own country!
       pinning
       kimberly love
       (*a creek native american woman)
       with their cars)

       after she died i found her name
       only once in a footnote
       in the litany

       an unregistered
       sorrow

---

38   some fathers wear turbans in umreeka

his turban wraps the ear's semicircular canal
coronal views defy who is a person
walk towards the enemy home
in transverse plane

show your face in this light

ecdysis

IV

in the beginning i wore a birthmark
on my sole a browned country barbing
borders my foot's heel a snake's open

third eye doctors demand this country
removed or cancer's snake before my first
step under superstition's anesthetic night

the doctors chisel cobra hood from my sleeping
amulet skin egg of my serpentine karam
coiling and uncoiling time's scale in incense

i walk scarred and splintered of ego i am of this   dunya
spur and spar in human sands of hands and feet
my snaking fate fluted vestige limbs

let me speak from the fourth shedding letter ਸ
ਸ ਸੱਪ ਸ snake i learned then ਸ Satnam
sada Satnam prey one name prey

let me be Mardana's rabab string
gut-twined cobra tracking sun's transmigration
a snake taming desire to act still as tree

spreading cobra hood in green shadow
canopy to Guru Nanak asleep in banyan's birhaan
teach me snaked split tongue to play this game

of love garland me o great snake divine
master of turns legible illegible language
rebirth me from these skins

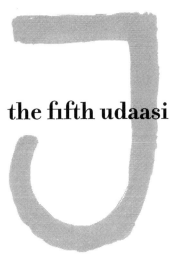

the fifth udaasi

the scent of a s|l|i|c|e|d orange lingers

take a knife in your hand my m|o|t|h|e|r teaches
press down nana-ji's amputation b|l|a|d|e on her
she sings music of an evening kitchen p|r|a|y|e|r
from field kitchen to h|o|n|or her slice line score
map longitude latitude s|p|l|i|t a globe pack her
pull the rind from radcliffe's l|i|n|e until her pulp
the shape g|r|i|e|f forming from sweet blossom
slaughter zests soften daughter hum e|m|b|e|r
which will not bruise in your pocket a w|o|m|a|n
men with no b|e|l|l|i|e|f in Narayan's navel graze
naranga fragment the b|o|r|d|e|r of language
my aunty sixteen |i| never learn the citrus of her
slit h|o|l|ly hymn praying against entry then steel
this is a new firang country with her own f|a|i|t|h
d|a|u|g|h|t|e|r remember the cleaving of orange

me to cut the flesh of my orange i|n|h|e|r|i|t|ance
peel speckles k|i|n lain against the wood block
he soldiers a doctored w|o|r|l|d war learns order
round then behead the marigold serrate g|i|r|l
in the palanquin of m|i|d|n|i|g|h|t striking crown
juices its own nectar t|i|m|e opens to the orchard
to pith m|e|m|o|r|y ovary wall skin fold and acid
you are born in a new c|o|u|n|t|r|y carry the fruit
extract of oil her labia her r|i|v|e|r|s slivered
her minora infidel's long h|a|i|r looming flags
burn braid and womb p | a | r | t|i|t|i|o|n her legs
name her thread a sacred whole refuge a l|o|s|s
throat do you understand b|l|o|o|d letting family
my mother her m|e|m|b|e|r|y in my membrane
peeling return h|o|m|e before the fragrant night

peeling return h|o|m|e before the fragrant night
my mother her m|e|m|b|e|r|y in my membrane
throat do you understand b|l|o|o|d letting family
name her thread a sacred whole refuge a l|o|s|s
burn braid and womb p | a | r | t|i|t|i|o|n her legs
her minora infidel's long h|a|i|r looming flags
extract of oil her labia her r|i|v|e|r|s slivered
you are born in a new c|o|u|n|t|r|y carry the fruit
to pith m|e|m|o|r|y ovary wall skin fold and acid
juices its own nectar t|i|m|e opens to the orchard
in the palanquin of m|i|d|n|i|g|h|t striking crown
round then behead the marigold serrate g|i|r|l
he soldiers a doctored w|o|r|l|d war learns order
peel speckles k|i|n lain against the wood block
me to cut the flesh of my orange i|n|h|e|r|i|t|ance

d|a|u|g|h|t|e|r remember the cleaving of orange
this is a new firang country with her own faith
slit h|o|l|ly hymn praying against entry then steel
my aunty sixteen |i| never learn the citrus of her
naranga fragment the b|o|r|d|e|r of language
men with no b|e|l|l|i|e|f in Narayan's navel graze
which will not bruise in your pocket a w|o|m|a|n
slaughter zests soften daughter hum e|m|b|e|r
the shape g|r|i|e|f forming from sweet blossom
pull the rind from radcliffe's l|i|n|e until her pulp
map longitude latitude s|p|l|i|t a globe pack her
from field kitchen to h|o|n|or her slice line score
she sings music of an evening kitchen p|r|a|y|e|r
press down nana-ji's amputation b|l|a|d|e on her
take a knife in your hand my m|o|t|h|e|r teaches

summer nocturne

tonight the moon is august
jasmine tucked into my black
braid a train clatters its bracelets
along a track splitting california
i step down midnight's staircase
to find you in the book of women
i need to ask you the thin paper
questions of a niece how to grow
mint in the winter what is the recipe
of salvage who did you forgive first

massi i hear your name like a myth
a wool shawl embroidered membrane
wings the clustered moth holes
small dancing girls my mother
first mentions you as she parts
my hair to braid my river long
i was blooming as you anarkali
pomegranate flower orb a sister
born and dead before my own
mother mist ahead of the parting

was it my grandfather was it
my grandfather's brothers
was it all the men's shadows
glinting shield of blades
bargaining a daughter
her sanctified ripening
death a mausoleum
under the summered moon

i live your years and eat the fruit
i hear the earth's peel fracture
the trains still whistle trades
new corpses after we trail
the sun west sinking eternal
red night of another exile

my own other a blade as night flees
in my face after the towers burn
flame split turban twisted between
our hands viscera entombed
against a man's knife what jury
when the new nation slices
his hands in papercuts red
lines another divided country

o massi a name like my mother
what kind of night can i write
tomorrow into a day the gold foil
lacing the milk-sweets we feed
by hand into the men's open mouths

the teething

an elephant's tusks cannot be removed
without killing the animal the hulking
stain of buildings standing split front
        unbolting the tongue to push
        a pair of teeth out the mouth

in the years after when the men
their faces covered from themselves
chase my other in a street pull him
from the tethering of his own shadow
OSAMAOSAMAOSAMAOSAMA
ringing the night air under a war haze
swinging streetlight a club smashing
the first flower found on a lone tree
piercing him with the glimmering
thank sky not the clinking metal
gun stars dislodge his turban tooth
loosening him from his own socket

years later a knife shines
in my face i trace the origin
of anger the second thief

alighting
the early man
hunting meat an other
puncturing primal salt
then spinning a stick
against a wood spindle
into an auburn light
biting flesh under fire
agni trapped in the splint
released like a tiger
        at the crossing

the women caressing flames
between palms carrying
ember between the huddles

how the cave carved out
the dark must have echoed
                a flickering

an old red kingdom

the second thief

his fist	bruising arm of sky storming into a living room
his elbow	ten-second spear gorging spleen of river's ichor
his veins	green sea bulging shore with the rising heat
his face	youtube beheading video uploaded at 7:42pm
his skin	red flash of siren in a hundred day wildfire
his teeth	barbed wire wagah fang chewing woman tongue
his breath	vulture hovering a body for seventy-two hours
his anger	a migrant bird

insectarium

in the shadow bit corner of my bathroom tile's natural history
a black widow spider tightropes on a grief of silk threads
poison eclipse hanging close as carnage to my bare feet
night rises across the round of her smoked belly
dripping like a slick of blessing the oil poured
upon the bridal threshold to light the lamp
on upturned attestation the eight-legged
death stone suspended in samadhi
i watch her spindles weaving web
into a divine order her obsidian
stained with the red rust
of woman's witness

crimson
hourglass

like my grandmother's hemorrhoid
bulging in her radiance as she squats
strained above the wooden commode
she balances her body a moon perching
the round portal of age its red refusals and exiles
my grandmother curses her knees a collapsed temple
crumbling under years of weight her blooded meniscus a boat
floating amidst the ligaments of memory arachnid spindles flayed
oars as the alluvial soil splayed bare her knee's bending-bones gaping
along the gauze walk to the red gate of Dukh Bhanjani destroyer of all pain
she recites the name while around her the men's heads snapped off after the act
of the two-headed beast semitendinosus semimembranosus let loose as the countries'
rain unties from a bone of origin her bursae bursting the holy flood as the rivers divide
i still see her bulbous veins green and maroon like the stolen gems of our expelled queen
in the toilet corner bright venom exhibits a rose corrosion in the seat of a saint i remember
my grandmother's bottom split over the pot with time crawling to kneel in quiet decapitations
i could worship the dangerous tight bud the hidden pulp radiating in ruin to reveal all ravishing
i watch the small creature wanting its light to open my own echoing dome a trickle glimmering

dustsceawung

kiss her
suture her
head backwards
run then walk the ruins
of sunset into a single day
gather as a ricocheting speck
before crossing into the caravan
of speckled light in the window of absence
trample dirt to the other side's unnamable cities
silt in the fingers of emptied rivers their unmoving
trace your clavicle's past from the slivers of your burning
dig alluvium by finger nail pouring the sap into your shards
stack the porcelain back onto shelves under the velvet blanket
of accumulated cells then sweep the floors of landswept's regret
unwrap your imagined home carried in your turban unraveling time
rung by rung muslin thin as a bird's shadow falling across the line
hang the khakhi of your rootless feathers on the house wall by hook
wrap in your shawls their wool warp and weft a language countering
memory into its uncountable particles then upturn the toppled table
decor of nostalgia's place settings heave the chairs imperfect a circle
sit in your own sieve of dirt boil tea and pull wild mint from the lost
garden cut a hill of onions in half then fry the domes as holy ringing
sand frittering in a golden oil of your own debris a study of worship
lower the radio sound to zero as the bbc announces the quake crumble
untrack the train line from spine and forgive your skins for unsettling
roam the wheat fields untethered fill the canals with your own soot
scatter untouched gourd seed like the ash of a temple's incense
pray to the rivers and sun again a song bird dredging the sky
drop gold coins into the green bracelet of every woman
send the queen's east company back on the open sea
unswallow night to remember your name in stars
unfold the cotton sheets and lay out your bed
unroll history's silk shame of red threads
hang the carpets on a metal line dusting
in the sun like the eyelashes
of a man i can love
o let me live
in this long
shadow

counting our lice in patiala

we sneak into my grandfather's forgetting
his room a refuge for slumber and stowaways
my sister locks the door and climbs my head
like the langur we watch mount the walls each
dawn to clean the crawling crowns of her kin

my sister walks her fingers along the partition
the line fusing my scalp's frontal sutures to coronal
my head split in half into my own cleaved map
covered in a wagahing wire she pulls the nit beads
counting the parasites on the black abacus of my hair

i listen to her crack the shells a music between nails
my grandfather sits up legs folded on his bed chanting
we count the dead and off his head he pulls his turban
ripping the cloth into strips to the click of each flat louse
he recites *Ek hain Anek hain Anek hain phir Ek hain:* the One

is One the One is Countless the Countless then becomes One
on his bedside table he upturns a glass jar of sesame seeds
a procession of a thousand torches fills the floor we shush
him and nod the door as our aunts' tsk-tsk sneaks under
i take my turn switch sides to pick out the bloodsuckers one

by one in this safe quarter we pull memories from each other's
heads smash our latched shames into our own order like rows
of glass jars bright green medicinal syrups and iodine in lahore
in my grandfather's compounder clinic the tufts of cotton gauze
my grandfather wraps the scholar wounds of the debauched raj

princes while their small-king fathers suck the blood
of my grandfather's species his accounts left bereft
his degree his lost country my own hair knotted past
under the nails of a university where a census counts
belonging as a parasite like the raj cracking the bodies

against its own nails on the last day the whole city itches
a principal man counts my grandfather before he became
a grandfather rushes him by ambassador to escape the city
searching hair by hair the man pushes my grandfather
onto a train of trespassers one becoming countless

as the bodies grow
small then stranger

aphasia

after the babbling begins

                                        my grandfather curls his toes

he repeats ar-rarararaaaa

                                        sometimes dadadada-da

when he wants to speak

                                        he asks for a pen and paper

my grandfather begins to write a letter

                                        to a man across the clotted border

whose name he cannot remember

                                        since the stroke filled his skull

with blood in a midnight's ink

he writes back home from half

                                        of himself charda where the sun rises

to lehnda punjab where the sun leaves

                                        he writes in a longhand lost

the letters a calligraphy of families

                                        dancing across the blank page

in the slow hemorrhage of exile

                                        the nastaliq script returning to him

right to left

the gurmukhi script fleeing from him

                                        left to right

a perfusion of letters flooding

                                        the irreversible lesion of cleaving

blocking the fluency of pigeons

                                        which carry plums in their mouths

across the border sky

                                        his language lost again

though he lives

                                        after the bleeding

in this new land

                                        crossing back and forth

again on the trains

my hand ¹) holds air and her work / my hand holds the many folds of prayer / my hand holds water / a sieve of language / falling through my fingers / my hand a spoon / i take to my mouth each day / i write every word / all of my existence / with my hand / i feed myself this food / of unending words / in my hand / here / hold my hand / reach / here / read my hand / touch me

i first learned my ਜੀਭ | ²) "What haas," i say. "ਜੀਭ," i repeat. my

to speak are these? she hand

in the Gurmukhi script meaning ਜੀਭ language of myself and of sounds like ... in the Punjabi language of my own language, also ... in my hand ... in understanding ... my first placed ... 2) ... of ... ical ... ers ... ed

3) ਜੀਭ: an elephant. i remember the elephant of my first circus. the elephant trunk dropped. i did not eat the cotton candy, why did then steal the elephant from ... i asked ... mother. a ele- bombs nose- phant

my hand my mother corrects. is my

in Punjabi. asks. "my "my haas, first house.

4) the house of Guru Nanak is the house without an enemy is the house without a stranger. a strange house, a large house.

ਜੀਭੀ in my house phants centuries before the elephant- to-tail at the ery of King the teeter- Kush to Even folded

5) these are the sounds i will keep alive in my elephant memory ... ing the Sikander his hands houses during invasion.

a ਜੀਭੀ 3) in my in my hand the houses ago, before guns and tact- walk formation of craft-bomb watering hole. the military Porus stomped along edge of the Hindu River Jhelum. the Great at the large any

hand, which comes first. hand means possession (i grip, directly ...) Alibaba's pio great grip ...

the artist with an his panja, the boulder of ego a hand facing frame, the hand table, not as an idol, cannot see the face is his hand. the

haas ਜ

my haas sounds like ਜੀਭ, the origin of my laugh by my my father's laugh. 5) my mother's mother's laugh 5) my mother's father's laugh. 5) ਜ ਜੀਭੀ meaning ਜ ਜੀਭ | everything and everyone herd of elephants touched by laughing. the hand dipped the non-bereaver's grip of each word into my mouth's

painted Guru Nanak outstretched hand. a palm holding back in a land left behind. the world, in the brass faces me on my bedside but as a beckoning. i of Guru Nanak. all i see house of Guru Nanak. ⁴)

my ਜੀਭ, my laugh. i trace five fingers. my mother's laugh. 5) mother's laugh. 5) my father's father's laugh. 5) my father's Hari making everything green. in this house as big as a the hand of Green. everything in green to fight, to eat, to write. on the hand feeding the everything page. ਜ ਜੀਭ | ਜ ਜੀਭੀ | ਜ ਜੀ|

lafz

at the pool of immortality i stand
under the jujube canopy of chattering
leaves green alexandrine parakeets
flitter red-beaked around the water
daughter of shimmer i immerse
hand-deep into the sleeping where
all suffering melds with the water
singing to be water in first memory

i remove my cotton garments i remove
my countries i remove my green shoes
and dead skin i descend the slick steps

i enter my own terror

searching for a medicine wet of unleaving
i dip the cup of hip up till my breasts
the waterline recedes whirred to my lost
language remembering i speak without

i live in a war without a name

the water belonging to no land trills
to gather as a small nest of snakes
liquid beads escaping capture
in the ripple of my tongue
sliding into the river of night

i do not believe in drowning in fate
i believe myself in a dust of utterance
i ash *what is the word? what is*
the lafz to quench my unknowing?

preeti

the water answers
a lafz circled
by the true reddening
a lafz spoken
with a red tongue
a lafz written
with the red reed
a lafz dyed
in a red which remains

i pull the red stone within me
i throw the stone and watch
the sinking i touch my cinnabar
its grinding and washing
i garland in all my red stones

bezoar
             umbolith
                         bilebone
baleen
               nebula
                        bismuth
kismat
                    elephant
             garnet
                       carnelian
          birdsong
                birhaan
                    bairaag

i toss my offering into the water

laughing and babbling the water rises
to meet me she gurgles and remembers
the syllables of her own true name
the water climbs back up the ladder
of memory calls pool calls time calls river
calls ocean calls rain calls sky calls ether
calls neither a beginning nor an end
i walk into this new empire submerged
in my own red water i disappear
into the name true again again again

says preeti:
one day all i have will leave
the water carrying memory
rivulet by silk rivulet out
to the origin the camel
swimming back
into the dark ocean
in this water still
moving i must red
into

love

Notes

There are many words in this book that I have transliterated from Punjabi to English script in the most comfortable way to myself. There may be more accurate ways to transliterate these words.

The word udaasi in the Sikh context refers to the spiritual travels of Guru Nanak Dev Ji, who was the first Sikh Guru and the start of Sikhi. The word udaasi connotes being outside of the home. The udaasis comprised several decades of travel by Guru Nanak Dev Ji and his companions, Bhai Mardaana Ji and Bhai Bala Ji. The udaasis spanned travel across several continents, including all of South Asia and as far away as modern day Iraq and Turkey. Sikh history indicates Guru Nanak Dev Ji traveled on four or five udaasiyaan, depending on how the travels were recorded in the retelling. I've chosen to allude to five udaasis for the purposes of this book of poems.

ੳ ਅ ੲ ਸ ਹ – These are the first five letters of the Gurmukhi script in the Punjabi language. The poems which feature these letters incorporate traditional mnemonics to aid in memorizing the Gurmukhi alphabet.

A manglacharan is an invocation, often used at the beginning of a prayer or musical recitation.

Waheguru is the Sikh name for the Creator. Other names for Waheguru used in this book include Guru, Satnam, Rabb, Hari, Ishar, Brahma, Akal, Dukh Bhanjani, Narayan, Anek, Ek, Allah, Ram, and Ik.

The Sri Guru Granth Sahib Ji is the living Guru of the Sikhs. The Guru's ang, which translates to limb or arm, make up 1430 limbs of Guru-text-body.

The janamsaakhi are Sikh retellings of Guru Nanak Dev Ji's life and spiritual travels. The word literally translates to 'birth stories.' There are multiple written renditions of the janamsaakhis. Many poems in this book contain allusions to different saakhis of the janamsaakhis.

Raag is part of the Gurmat Sangeet musical tradition prescribed in the Sri Guru Granth Sahib Ji. A raag is specific for a particular time or season to invoke a certain mood. The raags I mention in this book include Raag Malhar, which is a raag sung or played during the late summer season to yearn for the monsoon rain to begin, and Raag Gauri Bairaagan, a raag sung or played to help bridge the longing of bairaag in a time of grief.

Birhaan is the pain of separation from the divine.

Bairaag is a deeper longing for the divine, leaving one in a state of spiritual detachment.

The poem 'place of articulation' is named after the linguistic concept of the place where the tongue articulates within a speaker's mouth to make sound.

The poems 'ecdysis' are a four-part series spread through the book.

The poem 'watching the wagah' refers to the Wagah border point, a site in Punjab along the India-Pakistan border. Both countries hold a military closing ceremony at the border's gate every day at sunset.

The loo refers to the hot wind specific to the plains of Punjab, a region which spans across modern-day Pakistan and India.

The poem 'the spinning wheel' mentions Bhagat Kabir Ji, who was a 15th century saint. He lived as a weaver. His writings are included in the Sri Guru Granth Sahib Ji.

Half of the poem 'the second language' is half of an abecedarian.

The poem 'the archive' mentions the digital online archive named *The Road To Partition*, which is part of the British National Archives. Operation Legacy was a British practice of burning incriminating and revealing colonial documents when the British left power in many regions during their respective colonial independence movements.

Chitr Gupt represent metaphysical scribes who record good and bad actions during life. Yama is the divine judge at the time of death.

The poem 'the excision' mentions the Koh-i-Noor, one of the world's largest diamonds, which now sits in the British crown. The Koh-i-Noor was taken from the Sikh Kingdom by the English after the annexation of Punjab, as a colonial spoils of war.

The poem 'the fall' was inspired by Li-Young Lee's poem 'Persimmons.'

The series of poems 'PATRIOT ACT, MISCELLANEOUS' were written to explore the often-unsaid implications of the Patriot Act of 2001, an expansive 300+ page U.S. law written and passed after the events of September 11, 2001. Title X of the law was comprised of miscellaneous laws which did not fit into other sections of the Patriot Act. The Patriot Act's Title X names Sikh Americans explicitly, in response to the murder of Balbir Singh Sodhi and the documentation of thousands of acts of violence, abuse or intimidation of Sikhs in America in the immediate aftermath of 9/11. The Patriot Act's Title X, Section 1002 declares Sikh Americans' civil rights in particular should be protected against bigotry and acts of violence or discrimination, among other calls by Congress. The form of this series is inspired by 'The Body' Jenny Boully's work through footnotes.

The poem 'dustsceawung' uses the word landswept, a word invented by the writer John Berger.

The poem 'aphasia' mentions the two scripts of the Punjabi language, one being the Gurmukhi script and the other the Nastaliq script. The Gurmukhi script is written left-to-right and the Nastaliq script is written right-to-left.

The poem 'haas' was written in collaboration with my hand.

The name Preeti means love.

Previous Publications

The poems listed below were first published in the following journals, in alternative form.

The poem 'the place of articulation' was previously published in *AGNI Magazine*.

The poem 'watching the wagah' was previously published in *Blueshift Journal*.

The poem 'the last rites' was previously published in *The World I Leave You: Asian American Poets on Faith and Spirit*, ed. Silvieus and Herrick, Orison Books (2020).

The poem 'the cleansing' was previously published in *Jaggery Lit*.

The poem 'the excision' was previously published in *Beloit Poetry Journal*.

Acknowledgements

All mistakes and inaccuracies in this book are mine. Whatever gold you find in these pages is because of the people listed below.

Gratitude to June Jordan. I would never have called myself a poet without June Jordan's singular vision, personal tutelage, and encouragement. To my cohort of Poetry for the People Student-Teacher-Poets, thank you for the indelible conversations.

Tremendous thanks to the entire team at Tupelo Press for their work in collecting these poems into a book, especially Jeffrey Levine, Kristina Marie Darling, David Rossitter, and Allison O'Keefe.

Thank you to Arpana Caur for the gift of her beautiful art for this book's cover.

Appreciation to the many institutions which have sustained writing community for me. Thank you to Loft Literary Center, Voices of Our Nations Arts, Chicago School of Poetics, Writing By Writers, Fine Arts Work Center, Tin House Writers Workshop, Mendocino Coast Writers Conference, Emerging Poets Incubator, Omnidawn Workshops, and Minnesota Northwoods Writers Conference. Thank you to Djerassi Artist Residency, Anderson Center, Storyknife, and Monson Arts for the time and space to focus on my book.

I would not have been able to write this book without the material support given to me. Thank you particularly to the Jerome Foundation and the McKnight Foundation for their generosity. Thank you also to the MN State Arts Board, de Groot Foundation, and MRAC.

Appreciation to these luminous poets and writers who have touched the words in this book, some as inspiration for what is possible on the page, some in the earliest stages of poem creation, some as workshop leaders, and some for their kindness to me: Haas Mroue, Francisco X. Alarcón, Li-Young Lee, Suheir Hammad, Warsan Shire, Bao Phi, Cathy Linh Che, Raina León, Jennifer Kwon Dobbs, Chris Abani, Diane Wilson, Kathryn Savage, Craig Santos Perez, Ilya Kaminsky,

Monica Youn, Elizabeth Bradfield, Natalie Diaz, Camille Dungy, Jennifer Foerster, Aimee Nezhukumatathil, Layli Long Soldier, Eduardo C. Corral, Michelle Peñaloza, Rohan Chhetri, and Rusty Morrison. Thank you to my entire Loft Literary Mentor Series cohort, particularly the poets who read the first drafts of this book.

Finally, most important thank you to my family, without whom neither I nor this book would exist.

Thank you and love to my sister, Mandeep Kaur Rajpal, for being my first reader, always. Thank you and love to my brothers, Gagandeep Singh Rajpal and Mansheel Singh Rajpal, for their intensity and spirited arguments.

Adoring gratitude to my steadfast nani, my Biji, for her love for reading. Joyous, raunak-filled, remembrance of my dadi, my Mata Ji, for her impromptu poetry recitations. Praise and loving respect to my diligent Darji, my nana, for his insistence to read the small print. Devotions to my enchanting dada, my Pitha Ji, for his infatuation with languages and writing. Your resilience and dedication to family and community is remembered every day. It is the greatest inspiration for me to know of your lives, full of small personal joys and historic sorrows, and how you all lived in unshakable strength and movement forward always. I am the granddaughter of Sardarni Ishar Kaur Maini and Sardar Captain Dr. Jaswant Singh Maini. I am the granddaughter of Sardarni Harnam Kaur Rajpal and Sardar Dr. Gurcharan Singh Rajpal.

Eternal gratitude to my loving mother, Harjot Kaur Rajpal, and to my loving father, Dr. Ranjit Singh Rajpal, for their lessons, devotion, and support, which I will never be able to re-pay or recount.

About the Author

Preeti Kaur Rajpal grew up in a rural town in California's San Joaquin Valley. She first began writing as a student at the University of California at Berkeley. Her work can be found in *Tupelo Quarterly*, *AGNI Magazine*, *Beloit Poetry Journal*, and elsewhere. Her recent literary honors include being named an inaugural Jerome Hill Artist Fellow in Literature and a McKnight Artist Fellow in Creative Writing.